FROM A TO ZAY

The Indie Guide to Music Production

FROM A TO ZAY

The Indie Guide to Music Production

Xavier "Zaytoven" Dotson
With Tamiko Hope

Familiar Territory Book Publishing
Ellenwood, Georgia

FROM A TO ZAY
The Indie Guide to Music Production
Published by:
Familiar Territory Book Publishing
Ellenwood, Georgia
zaytovenbeats@yahoo.com

Xavier Dotson, Publisher / Editorial Director
Yvonne Rose/Quality Press.info, Production Coordinator
Printed Page, Cover Format and Interior Design
Jerome "Perion" Hunter, Cover Designer

© Copyright 2015 Xavier Dotson
ISBN #: 978-0-9961654-0-2
Library of Congress Control Number: 2015935587

Dedication

I'd like to dedicate this book first and foremost to God for blessing me with the talent to create music and enjoy the life that I'm living now. His love and guidance have never failed me.

Acknowledgements

I would like to take the time to acknowledge my family, especially my parents, wife and children, as well as my brother and sister who've all encouraged me every step of the way. They have been supportive and patient with me over the years, keeping me grounded and I'm happy to be able to share this incredible journey with them.

To my church families in California and Georgia, which is where my passion began for playing the drums, organ and piano and still continues. I appreciate being given the opportunity to express myself through the gift of music.

To Danny "Humble G" Jefferies for his encouragement and expertise during my trek into the world of book publishing.

This guide wouldn't be possible if it wasn't for the vision and writing skills of my longtime publicist and book collaborator Tamiko Hope. I'd also like to show my sincere gratitude to Yvonne Rose, Director of Quality Press, for her editing magic and publishing expertise. Special thanks to Jerome "Perion" Hunter for the dope cover art he created.

And lastly, I'd like to thank all of you who invested in this guide. It is my sincere hope that you will use the content found in these pages as a valuable tool to make all of your music production dreams and more, come to fruition.

—Xavier "Zaytoven" Dotson

Contents

Preface

I started my career in the music business like most R&B artists—in the church. My mom sang in the choir and my dad was a minister, so being in church was like my second home. As an overly hyper kid, my folks thought there was no better way to channel my creative energy than with an instrument, preferably the organ or the drums. This was something I could bang on instead of the pews. They were both made to be struck with force, which was the perfect pastime for a 10 year-old. I could be as loud as I wanted, because at least I was making noise for God, right? I took a strong liking to the drums, but I really connected with the keys on the piano and organ.

My mom was one of the first people to recognize my raw talent and tried enrolling me in piano lessons to help refine my self-taught style, but I quit after a couple of sessions. There was something I liked about figuring out things and sounds on my own that really kept me interested. I enjoyed playing the way I wanted to play and coming up with my own melodies; and giving myself the freedom to mess up and learn at my own pace. Looking back over my life, I was born to be an entrepreneur, a self-starter, a hustler. I enjoy the grind and seeing how much I can accomplish. I continued to practice the piano and organ until I was offered a full-time position to play in the church, which I still do 'til this day, although it's a different church.

My life story is my motivation for writing this book. It comes from me wanting to help young, gifted people who have the skills and passion for music, but no direction on how to get there or even where to start. It's the exact same spot that I started at. Moving cross-country from the Bay area at 23-years-old to Atlanta, where the only people I knew were my immediate family, was a challenge. I had to basically start all over again and make new connections, although being a military brat, new beginnings was my specialty.

In doing so, I mastered a whole new approach to developing relationships with people and making things happen from the bottom. Not only did I relocate physically, but my sound experienced a transition as well. I had to figure out how to make my beats more southern-friendly, but still fit my flavor because Atlanta had a whole different type of sound than in San Francisco. It forced me to learn new styles of producing, in addition to new techniques in meeting the right people who could help me with my career. Doing it that way taught me every aspect of the business; the roles and responsibilities of industry types, what I could do on my own, the essential people I needed to put on my team, how much I needed to pay for things, how I was going to get paid and the list goes on and on.

From A to Zay: The Indie Guide to Music Production is years of successes and failures, and how you can duplicate the things I did right and avoid the things I did wrong. Let's get ready to go down the list of everything you need to know about music production (and perhaps life) from A to Zay.

—Xavier Dotson

Introduction

I would be amiss not to first mention my faith in God, the support of my family and friends, and also my belief in myself, which have all served as strong motivating forces in helping me accomplish what I have thus far. I get asked questions all the time about how indie producers like myself can get their music out there. That is one of the main reasons why I wanted to do a book like this.

I feel like, not only is this project about my professional journey, but it's just as much about life lessons as well. This was the best way to respond to a lot of those questions that I've been asked over the years. *From A to Zay: The Indie Guide to Music Production* helps me to answer them in a way that allows me to explain in greater detail the basic principles that have worked for me from A to Z. This is the road I took to get me to the point that I am at today.

Of course everyone will have a different success story experience (as they should), but I feel at the end of the day there are only a handful of philosophies that if learned and practiced consistently, will guarantee that whatever you are aiming for you will surely hit.

An intelligent person aims at wise action, but a fool starts off in many directions.

—Proverbs 17:24

1. Action

As you know, I grew up in the church—my pops was a minister and my mom sang in the choir; so when I wasn't in school, I was in church. Not only did I grow up as a preacher's kid, but I was also a military brat. We lived in Germany for a while, which is where I was born and ironically the birthplace of Beethoven, the classic pianist where my professional name comes from (more on that later).

When I was still a baby, my dad got transferred to San Francisco, the Bay area to be exact, and that's where my journey began. Because I was in church so much and being a typical boy that gets into everything, my mom made me get involved in a church activity to channel my energy. Since I liked to beat on the church pews, the drums seemed like the move and I liked playing them but they didn't hold my attention. I was drawn to the piano. I was fascinated by the various sounds you could make by pressing a different key. I could sit still for hours experimenting with what noises the black keys made, as well as the white ones, while creating a melody. I was hooked. Of course I didn't know what I was doing exactly, but I began spending all my free time trying to learn how to play. Within months, I got good and eventually started playing the organ for the church every Sunday. Music became my life. I practiced nonstop, not because I had to, but because I wanted to. It was as important as eating and breathing for me. I'm grateful to my mom for taking **action** and insisting that I get involved in music; I've been playing the keys ever since.

God responds to bold action. When I got in high school, I began using my hands in another way—cutting hair. I can't explain where the desire came from, but it did; and I didn't waste time trying to figure it out. I acted. I borrowed some clippers and used my younger brothers as guinea pigs to see if I was any good at it. An important thing for producers, artists or anybody trying to pursue a goal is to remember that, in order to get started, you have to take **action**; and I will go a step further and say *immediately*. In Ecclesiastes 11:4 it says, *"If you wait for perfect conditions, you will never get anything done."*

How many people do you know who've been working on the same beats or a mixtape project for a few years but haven't put any work out into the marketplace because they're trying to perfect it or feel they're lacking something? They get 'ready' and 'set' but they never 'go,' the most important part. It's always going to be something to improve upon but the lesson here is to do the best you can with what you have, exactly where you are and put it out into the world. I practiced on my brothers until I got solid enough to start cutting hair in the neighborhood and moved on to my high school friends. I would charge anywhere from $5 to $10 depending on if somebody wanted designs or something out of the ordinary. But the thing that amazed me was that I made a decision to cut hair, took immediate **action** and a month or so later, was getting compensated for something I enjoyed doing. If you don't put what you do out there (take **action**), you'll never got out there either.

Once I became fully aware that you could actually turn your hobby into a career, I knew that entrepreneurship was for me. The bonus in my discovery was that I could get paid doing what made me happy; something that came natural to me although making a ton of money wasn't a big motivation. I didn't really have a desire at the time to be super rich and still don't, I just wanted to be able to meet my responsibilities and not be burdened by debt. While I was crunk, my parents weren't thrilled about me choosing entrepreneurship over going to school. They wanted stability for me. I expected them to be a little wary of my approach to conquering the real world, but I knew in my heart what I wanted and needed to do. I had to **act**.

Act to produce results. While I was known as the neighborhood hair-cutter, I was also still doing music. My high school didn't have a band but I and a homeboy formed one literally. We fulfilled a need, a purpose; we took **action**. I was on the keyboard and he was on the drums; just the two of us. We played in the stands at all the home football games. We'd play whatever the most popular songs were on the radio at the time and we'd have everybody going crazy. As God would have it, a guy by the name of "JT the Bigga Figga" was at one of the games and approached me about going into the studio with him. This was around '98 and JT was truly a Bay area legend. He had a major label deal at the time and his name was buzzing pretty heavy in the streets because he was working with a lot of different guys. By him coming up to me, wanting to work and do business, it was like confirmation that I was on to something; I just didn't know what. JT believed in my musical talent and knew that if he could show me how production equipment worked, that I'd be a dope producer. I was a little uneasy because I'd never produced anything before but I didn't want to use that as an excuse. I wanted to at least try.

JT called a few weeks later and asked me to come to his studio. I took **action** ASAP. I didn't want to wait or postpone. Dale Carnegie said, *"Inaction breeds doubt and fear. **Action** breeds confidence and courage. If you want to conquer fear, do not sit home and think about it. Go out and get busy."* JT showed me how things worked in the studio a few times and he'd leave me in there by myself for hours. Week by week, I'd sit there and figure it out until it all started coming together. Like everything I had mastered at that point in my life, I approached it gorilla-style and learned the technical ropes of music production.

Act like the producer (or person) you want to be. Every opportunity I had, I was in the studio but I felt like I needed something or someone to gauge my progress. I needed a producer mentor but I didn't know any personally. I decided to find a producer who was 'the' best or one of the best in my book and began to mimic their style. I chose DJ Quik. Of course he was from Cali and at that time West coast artists like Dre, Snoop, Ice Cube, Nate Dogg, Warren G and E-40 were all popping; and my beats were centered around that whole Soul and Funk Rap era. I felt like I had graduated from college when I created a beat that sounded as if DJ Quik made it; that's when I knew I had something special.

Now it was time for me to move on and put my spin on tracks. **Once you have mastered your mentor's sound, start adding your own stamp to the track.** That will make it your own. For me, it was my drum pattern. Mostly all of my beats have that signature sound to it and it's something I've become known for and also my Zaytoven piano tag at the beginning of my tracks. There are even websites out there dedicated to creating my style; it's all very flattering and I don't take offense to it. I look at it like we all have to start somewhere, but you have to take **action**. It's not good enough to say you are *going to* do something or simply write down your intentions or read a book like this and not apply the principles. You need to get to doing.

As soon as I got confident in my beat-making abilities, I would make cassette tapes at JT's studio and take them home for guys from school to come by and rap to. I always had an ear for that "it" factor quality in rappers so I knew who could flow and who I thought would fit my sound. I would recruit dudes from the basketball team or friends that I heard spit in between classes or at parties. It's pretty cool for me to look back on that time and see how I've been developing talent since I was a teenager. My passion for production grew and I became known as the go-to guy for a cut and beats.

The key is to take the smallest of **action** steps every day and God will put the right people and situations in your life to get you to your destiny. Let me repeat that. Work on something every single day that will bring you closer to your goal. Stop wondering what you can do and start acting.

I'm just Zaying…I got the name Zaytoven a year later from a rapper named Forest who used to buy beats from me. He'd pay me whatever price I told him and say *'Zay go in and make me a beat; whatever you feel like.'* We both had a love for music, so he trusted me. One day Forest said, *'you play the piano so good you sound like Beethoven. I'm gonna call you Zaytoven.'* It was the perfect name being that my name is Xavier (X-zay-v-er). People were already calling me 'Zay' but I didn't use it then since I had already started a buzz using the name Xavon (Zay-von) and that's who people knew me as in the Bay.

What do you mean, 'If I can'? Jesus asked. Anything is possible if a person believes.

—Mark 9:23

2. Believe

After years of playing in the church and clocking countless hours in the studio practicing and steadily trying to improve, my name started circulating in the streets as a solid producer. Around this time, I'd graduated high school and my parents relocated to Atlanta, although I decided to stay in the Bay to build on the momentum I was getting. But it was hard. I was cutting hair and making beats but I had more bills than money.

There's a scene in *Birds of a Feather* where my car won't start, which was just a small part of a bigger true story. My car actually broke down while I was going through the toll of the Bay Bridge; one of the longest in the world. I drove a bucket like most people in the Bay; at that time nobody cared about flashy cars. And like anybody who drives a hooptie, you know exactly what makes yours tick. In my case, I had already rigged it to start and knew I wouldn't be able to make a complete stop at the toll booth because it would cut off if I did and I wouldn't be able to start it back up. So as I rolled up to the booth in neutral, I had to also apply pressure to the gas pedal so it wouldn't idle down. But while I was balancing the brakes and gas and trying to pay the toll operator, I let my foot off the gas. And that was it.

I tried to crank it back up a few times but I knew it wasn't going to start. As God would have it, there was a tow truck in another lane that came over and bumped my car across the bridge to get me out of the way. Keep in mind that I barely had enough money to even pay the toll so I couldn't have it towed to a shop. I was able to roll off the bridge and where it stopped is where I left it.

I walked to the nearest bus stop to get home. Believe it or not, I enjoyed those simple times in my life taking public transportation because I got a chance to meditate on everything I wanted to accomplish. I had a lot of time to think too because I never knew when my car would act up and leave me stranded. I remember it breaking down on me just when I left the studio after I had stopped at a gas station. It was so late, or rather so early in the morning, that I just slept in the car. I had my pit bull with me so I didn't worry too much worry about anybody messing with me. That scenario of breaking down late at night happened a few more times and in each instance I'd chill out and lay down in my car until somebody could come scoop me early that morning, or I'd take the bus.

Believe in yourself first. I wanted to stay in the Bay because my music career was just starting; but I also wanted to build a studio of my own. I was renting a room in the home of my pastor so I couldn't just set up a studio in his house and have people coming in and out. It had been 2 years since my parents moved to Atlanta and I was making some progress in my career; but the cost of living in San Francisco wasn't allowing me to make the kind of moves I needed to make in order to further my career. My parents offered me the basement of their house to use as a studio and I decided to take them up on their offer. In order to grow, I knew I had to move.

I was a little nervous about leaving but I **believed** that God had something better for me. Once I made the decision to relocate to the south, I put a plan together on what I needed to do before I left the Bay. Every dollar I earned from playing at church, selling beats and cutting hair went towards production equipment. I would put each piece on layaway and every time I paid off an account, I'd have it shipped directly to my mom's house. I even got a job unloading trucks to pay off everything as fast as I could. During this period in my life, I didn't have much time or money to do anything else; but I was ok with that because I **believed** in me.

Having done those things as a young guy myself is the reason why I don't accept excuses; nor do I take people seriously when they tell me why they can't do something. If you want anything bad enough, you'll find a way to make it happen. Your **belief** in yourself will force you to take action; and if you don't feel that way, you may need to evaluate what your life purpose is and focus on your self-esteem.

I would make music even if I wasn't getting paid. I feel the same way about barbering. Those are my passions in life. I can't merely just think about those things, I have to do them and I strongly suggest you adopt the same mentality. There will be sleepless nights, plenty of times when you have to deal with the politics of the business that make you want to quit, money disputes, contract disagreements, industry folks not **believing** in you, artists who get the big head after they get a hit record with you, times when you have more dreams than money. In other words you will be put in situations that you'd rather not be in; but have to deal with them anyway, all for the sake of keeping your dream alive. I can't tell you how many times I've had no sleep, had the flu, had family issues on my mind; but have gone into the studio anyway, hosted a party anyway, attended an event anyway, invested and lost my own money all because I don't look at what I do as a job or even a career.

My work is as much a part of my life as the blood in my veins. When you **believe** you can, you can. When you **believe** you can't you can't. You get to decide who and what you **believe** in. Choose you.

Believe in the God-factor. The **belief** I had in my plan and in God is what guided my steps. The first thing I did when I got to Atlanta was enroll in barber college and secure a job playing the organ at church. I've never been one to sit around and wait for things to happen. I also wanted to have money coming in to pay my way and that included giving my folks something on the bills. Just like being in the church led me to play the organ, the barber shop gave me a network of people that led me to artists. In the usual barber shop way, there was a lot of talk amongst all of us, most of it about music.

It was the early 2000s and the south was on straight trap music with TI and Young Jeezy being the biggest rappers in the streets. The beats were melodic and hard, but straightforward. In the Bay, my sound was real sophisticated and complex, which is what I became known for. But since I was in a new city and would be working with different people, I wanted a fresh start as well. I adopted the name Zaytoven and decided to switch up my sound in the process.

Before I left the Bay I heard this song called "Ha" by an artist named Juvenile and it changed my whole perspective on rap music. He changed my ear because, up until then, I was a fan of artists that were very lyrical, almost poetic with their words and real intentional with their flow. However, Juvenile was the first artist I heard rap; but it didn't really sound like he was rapping. He just rode and finessed the beat. I really liked it and wanted to simplify my beats to cater to artists like that; artists that could jump on a track and swag it out. But that in itself takes a special skill. I knew an artist like that had to have a confident flair like Juvenile to give the music that edge to make it **believable**. So I had come to Atlanta knowing what type of artists I would cater to and what kind of beats I would create.

Believe in others. Through those barber shop conversations, I also learned that there were a couple of guys in class who rapped and I invited them over to the house to record. Of course the word spread overnight. One day, a guy by the name of Radrick Davis came to the house after someone told him about my studio and that I made beats. He fell through several times to check me out before bringing his nephew over. I thought his nephew was alright but I just didn't feel a connection. But Radrick was real persistent about his nephew, so they came over to the house pretty regularly; but something else was taking place in the basement that I couldn't explain at the time, or predict. Radrick would write the rhymes for his nephew, go into the booth, rap what he just wrote and then his nephew would go behind him to record.

I started to take a personal interest in Radrick. I had a feeling he was the artist I'd been looking for. Everything about him said 'star' to me—his words, his flow, his delivery, his attitude, even his look. After a few weeks, I expressed my interest in working with him but he didn't take rapping seriously. He was really trying to put his nephew on. But there's something to be said about the power of being behind the mic. The more he got in the booth, the more confidence he gained and he started to **believe** that he had some kind of undeveloped talent. It was going to be my job to keep bringing it out of him.

For me, you can be the main man on the charts; but if I don't have that feeling that moves me on the inside when we're working, I'd rather not work with you. Of course there will be occasions when you produce for people you may not be 100% sure of, and that's just part of the job; but when you find those special few that stir up your spirit, go with it. Go for broke. That's **belief** and that faith can change your life.

After those first few times Radric recorded on his own, he began coming to the studio so much and got so good at it that before long we had enough material for a mixtape. Even though I knew a lot of people wouldn't be able to see my vision because he wasn't the most articulate or the best rapper I'd heard, I **believed** in him. It was the way he made simple words sound good and how he put them together and said them. I just **believed** he was going to be the man to put me in the game in a major way. The music industry is all about whose name is hot, but my approach was different.

I didn't want to run around trying to catch up with guys that had already made it. I knew that they would get more shine than me on the record. My mission was to find a guy I **believed** in, which happened to be Radric, blow him up, and in turn I'd blow up. Motivational speaker John Maxwell talked about the principle of helping people get what they want, and in turn you will get everything you want. And being a spiritual guy, I **believed** and still **believe** in that principle; give first, in order to receive.

Ask yourself this question until you get an answer: *'what is that one thing I can do right now, right where I am with what I have that will jumpstart my career?'* As soon as you discover what that is, act immediately! For me, it was **believing** in an unknown guy off the street with no music experience and working tirelessly to make a hit single with no promise of anything happening.

Radric Davis became my main focus and he turned out to be arguably one of the biggest names in southern Hip Hop. If you keep the faith, stay committed and do the work, all the success you want will come to you without it being forced and that's the kind you want. In the words of Napoleon Hill *"whatever the mind can conceive and **believe**, it can achieve."*

I'm just Zaying...Michael Jordan **believed** in himself after getting cut from his high school basketball team...Colonel Sanders founded KFC at 65 years old using his social security check because he **believed**...In 1984 Steve Jobs was fired from Apple and we all know how that turned out. **Believe!**

*In the beginning God created the heavens and
the earth.*

—Genesis 1:1

3. Create

Now that I had found my protégé, the next step was to **create** a star.
Radrick Davis became known as Gucci Mane. It's common knowledge
that I don't like a whole lot of extra-ness in my life so it only made sense
to apply that philosophy to our movement. We kept our plan simple;
we'd out-work every artist that was hot in the streets or on the radio.
The way we were grinding, averaging 18 hour days, Gucci might as well
had lived at my house. He'd knock on my door at 6 in the morning after
we'd just stopped working at 3 AM to record more music. He was like a
machine, we both were. We ate music for breakfast, lunch and dinner.

He'd usually write in the mornings or record whatever he wrote the night
before; but it didn't really matter to me as long as we were **creating**. I
knew that if we just kept recording and recording and recording, we'd
eventually **create** something special. And that's exactly what happened.
It was 2004 and the record was "So Icy" although it didn't get popping
until a year later, which brings me to an invaluable lesson: you must
always stay **creating**.

Just because you make one hit record doesn't mean you stop or slow
down. It's actually the time when you need to mash the gas and go! In
this industry, you're only as relevant as your last hit, so you have to learn

to stay **creating**. And in order to **create**, you must also act. They go hand in hand. What use is it to **create** a catalog full of music and then never put it out or do anything with it? And trust me, nobody really cares about you when you first start out, so don't get bummed about people not paying you any attention; you have to **create** it. And the best way to get folks to listen is to **create** a demand.

Create a presence. When I got settled into my new life in Atlanta, I stayed in different clubs listening to the records the DJs were playing, in order to soak up the vibe and take that energy back home and work. I was also trying to meet as many music people as I could to **create** a presence. You've got to stay visible and be seen on the scene at the right spots. Every city has those places that are the known spots to be at; so go to those events that will serve you and your purpose. While you have to **create**, you must also go to the people to be seen and heard. And I'm not talking about just handing out business cards and CDs at the clubs. That's been done. Just because you may pass out a few cards and boxes of your product, don't think your music is going to just fall in the hands of somebody that can help take you to the next level.

I realize it can happen and has happened but that shouldn't be your only form of marketing. It halfway worked back when I was coming up but that's not considered real grinding today. Grinding is when you pave a road where there was just dirt. I don't care to hear people say things like, *"if I could just get a Zay beat, I'd be on," "if I could get hooked up with a superstar manager, I'd really take off"* or *"if I had more money to book studio time, I'd be outta here."* Those are all excuses, plain and simple. You can't stand in front of a fire and demand heat. You've got to put the wood in first before it will produce what you want.

In the same way, you must **create** your own opportunities. J. Cole moved from North Carolina to New York on the hopes of meeting Jay Z, which he eventually did. He even learned how to make his own beats when nobody would give him any. He **created a presence**, not excuses. Excuses are easy and have no value.

The group Migos put out a YouTube video of them rapping over one of my beats where they repeatedly shouted me out throughout the whole song. It caught my attention and everyone else's too. They **created a presence.**

You've got to separate yourself, while staying true to who you are in the process and work in your area of strength. I'm all for growing because we should push ourselves and set high goals; but if you're in this business just to get a check, you might blow up at first, but you'll burn out fast. This industry chews up folks who jump in it for the cameras and all the flexing that goes along with it; but eventually they get eaten up. I never did any of this for a dollar. When me and Gucci were spending all our time in the studio, our goal was never to make a hit record per se, we just enjoyed doing music together, which is why I think we made it. We never sat around talking about getting radio play, we just worked and networked and it all happened organically.

Create your blessings. Music and barbering have always been what I loved to do naturally, whether I was earning money from it, or not. There was a point in my career when I did both for free, but I looked at it like I was investing in myself. I have made the most money and enjoyed the fruits of my labor through the gift of using my hands. I've always focused on what I'm good at, but I've also constantly sought ways to build upon my blessings.

I'll touch on the subject again a little later in the book, but the movie *Birds of a Feather* came about because I took what I was good at and channeled it in a different way. I've always wanted to score a movie but nobody was knocking down my door to give me the opportunity to do so. With the help of my business partner Al Nuke, he wrote a script based loosely on my life and had me star in it; and I also provided the music for the film we **created**.

The whole key to my success, besides the obvious (God, faith, family) has always been my consistency to keep **creating**, whether that's making beats, writing hooks, scoring films or coming up with ideas to further promote something I'm involved in. Most people want the fame and the trappings of success without sacrificing anything. In this business or in anything you do, there's a price to pay to get what you want. Whatever is easy usually doesn't have a whole lot of value to it; anybody can have it.

That's why I wanted to tell my story, for people to know that the Zay they see today is Xavier Dotson; the one who rode the bus, worked unloading trucks and used layaway plans to get to where he is. Writer P.D. James sums it up best by saying, *"God gives every bird his worm, but He does not throw it into the nest."* There are blessings all around you, no mater where you are in life; but you must be willing to look for them, and by look, I mean **create**.

I'm just Zaying... If you want to create more income, you need to create more money-making opportunities. I like to take an hour or two at the top of my week to brainstorm on ways to increase my earning potential.

Ask and it will be given to you; seek and you will find; knock and the door will be opened to you.
—Matthew 7:7

4. Discover

Gucci and I had developed a one-of-a-kind chemistry that was nothing short of a miracle. It reminded me of Dre and Snoop, Toomp and TI, Timbaland and Missy. Even though we were from two completely different backgrounds and lived vastly different lifestyles, we connected creatively and that's why were able to work so well together. We each brought something special to the table to create a fresh and unique sound, which leads me to a key to success. Once I had established a name with Gucci, I continued hitting up the same clubs to **discover** that next star. You can never get too comfortable in life and especially not in the entertainment business where a new star is born every second. What kept me motivated and still does is knowing that it's always someone out there grinding just a little bit harder and working a little bit longer than me, ready to take my spot.

Don't get me wrong, there's enough success to go around for everybody but you have to take advantage of your name buzzing in the street while you have the spotlight. I heard a quote that says *"he who has the mic has the power"* and I couldn't agree more. It's wise to set up your next play while you're relevant in the game, while people are familiar with your name and waiting to see what your next move is going to be. Once you've established your buzz, that's the ideal time to get to that next level. For me, it was **discovering** other unknown talent.

Discover Talent. I met Yung LA at the Libra, a popular east Atlanta club during an open mic night they had every Thursday. It was the kind of place where if you rapped in there you felt like a star; you had made it. I'd go with Gucci all the time and meet different artists on the come up. On one particular night, Yung LA was performing and I had somewhere else to be, but he pleaded with me to stay. I didn't stick around, but we crossed paths several weeks later when I went to sell some beats at somebody's home studio. He started freestyling and no lie, he made the hairs on my arms stand up and I was moved to work with him. He was one of those guys that just had something different. I also met OJ Da Juiceman around the same time. He'd come over to the house and we'd record like crazy and eventually came up with some heat.

I have always enjoyed the **discovery** process. As I mentioned earlier, it's easy to want to work with an established name; but when you **discover** a coal-type of artist, give them a lot of heat and turn them into a diamond, that's what gets you noticed. Before "So Icy" blew up in '05, I was **discovering** and snatching up these new rising stars and working with them. I'd go to the clubs and open mics with Gucci and be on stage with him when he performed, since I made all the beats. I knew I needed to stay visible and for people to know me so I could **discover** and be **discovered**. I also went out because I always wanted to deal directly with the artists and have my own relationships.

After all of the hype surrounding "So Icy" you would assume that I was the busiest producer in the south, but that wasn't the case. Nobody called, nobody was looking for me, labels weren't hitting me up to work with their artists. The controversy surrounding the record overshadowed Gucci and me. Gucci had the biggest song out and nobody was rocking with him in Atlanta. At this time all I'm known for is Gucci, so nobody was rocking with me either. There was no instant success. Jeezy had the streets locked down and it seemed like the whole city was a fan of him, BMF and that movement.

Gucci was an outcast. As a result of all of this, I never experienced that "I got a hit record" feeling. That never happen for me, even 'til this day. We didn't really benefit as much as we could have, or should have, from "So Icy's" popularity. If you trace every song I've done throughout my career that's been big, I've had an issue with all of them. There hasn't been one song where things went smooth. With "So Icy" Gucci and Jeezy, I had issues; with "Make the Trap Say Aye" there were internal issues between me, OJ and his management; with "Papers", Usher was going through divorce drama; and with "Versace", Drake wasn't a part of the video.

But I recognize that all these experiences are just part of the journey; and it's my story. Maybe labels didn't kick down my door because I was independent, the artists who I recorded with were indie; or perhaps it was because I had no manager. But I wasn't hard to find. What I did have was publishing companies, street guys and new artists wanting to work with me, but not labels.

When 2008 and 2009 rolled around, I had so many songs on the radio, none of that mattered that much. There were countdowns on the Atlanta stations that were dedicated to my records and the artists I **discovered**. Back then there weren't as many producers, especially out of Atlanta. It was me, Shawty Redd, Nitti and Drumma. During that era, artists usually worked with one producer, so every beat on their mixtape had a certain vibe to it.

Now you might have a project that's got 14 songs by 14 different producers. I'm grateful to have come up at the time I did, doing an artist's entire project, because it helped to brand me. I did mixtapes with the new guys I **discovered** and as they established a buzz, so did I. History has shown that it's a proven success formula. Look at Dre and Snoop, Timbaland and Missy, Toomp and TI.

When people think of me, they attach me to Gucci. We established a sound together. Through **discovering** talent, these artists gave me my name and got me in the game.

I'm just Zaying… I remember when "So Icy" started getting club play; hundreds of people were singing all the words. I can't describe that feeling. The only other song that resonates with me like that is "Versace." They actually sound like the same song to me. I've made a lot of hits in the last decade, but in all those years only "So Icy" and "Versace" have made me feel a certain type of way.

While we were with you, we used to tell you, "Whoever refuses to work is not allowed to eat." In the name of the Lord Jesus Christ we command these people and warn them to lead orderly lives and work to earn their own living.
—2 Thessalonians 3: 10, 12

5. Earn

Coming up in the Bay where everybody was so independent and kinda just doing their own thing, I never wanted to be a part of the industry machine. I didn't want to get in bed with folks I didn't know and people who weren't around when I was living check to check and riding the bus. I've always been content with the money I **earned**, handling business on my own. I never had that *"I gotta take my career to the next level"* mindset; although I always strive to be a better person, which positively impacts everything else in my life. There was a point when I considered getting a manager, but after I found out they got 20 percent of everything coming in, I didn't want that. And I'll tell you why.

Earn your spot. I enjoyed a great run where everything started happening for me through word of mouth. Any rapper or anybody you could think of approached me for beats and all that was accomplished without a manager. I had **earned** a name in the industry that cut out the middle man because I had built my reputation on being an approachable guy. I made it a point to be easily accessible and you don't need a manager or a team to do that. I was never one of those guys that had to be roped off in VIP or didn't go to hood clubs or had security around me or a huge entourage. People respect that about me.

Everybody's different in how they do business; but by me going out so much I had developed personal relationships with people, which took away the traditional business model for having a manager. I'm also a very hands-on type of person anyway. I like to talk to people on the phone and in person and if I want to do a song with someone I want to be able to reach out to them. I like for an artist to come to the studio and we just hang out and vibe together. Nobody put me in touch with the artists I worked with; I found them, therefore I never felt that burning desire to have a manager.

Some people don't like to mingle and move around or set up studio time; but doing it this way has given me much more leverage than if I had a manager finessing my situations. It creates more opportunities. When managers are involved, it can complicate things; but if someone is dealing with me, they feel a personal connection and there won't be any extra-ness. I had heard a lot of artists complaining about how they had to wait for their manager to cut their check and when I started seeing those things for myself I didn't want to have any of those issues. Keep in mind that this is my approach and what has worked best for me and my needs. There are some reputable entertainment managers out there, I know a few of them; so you must consider what kind of person you are and what's important to you.

You've got to have an attorney to look over contracts and sign paperwork; and for me, mine is almost like my manager. I go out and put the deals together and he makes sure my interests are protected. I prefer having people around me that serve a purpose and **earn** their spot. Because of my go-getter attitude, I respect those that don't mind putting in the work first. Our rewards in life like peace of mind, money, homes, excellent health and vacations will always match our dedication. If you don't like what you've been getting, take a look at what you've been giving. What have you **earned?** When you **earn** your spot, it makes the process much more rewarding for you and you feel good about the people around you. Trust me.

*I'm just Zaying…*Proverbs 13:11 confirms **earning** by saying, *"The more easily you get your wealth, the sooner you will lose it. The harder it is to* ***earn****, the more you will have."* **Earn** your title, money, relationships, good health, reputation, respect, etc. If it's too easy there isn't a lot of value in it.

But if someone doesn't provide for their own family, and especially for a member of their household, they have denied the faith. They are worse than those who have no faith.

—1 Timothy 5:8

6. Family

The clubs I used to frequent when I was starting out were the dirtiest, grimiest, hole in the wall establishments you'd find. But it was also the very reason I would go. The outside of the club was a real representation of what was going on inside. A lot of the people in there were on powder, pills, dope and every other type of drug you could name; but those were the places where authentic music was coming from, music they didn't play on the radio. You would hear what was next before the mainstream caught on and that's why I enjoyed being there. I was able to jump on the trends before they became a trend.

Have family values. I wasn't a father and husband when I moved to Atlanta; that came a few years later. But a lot of people have asked me how I've remained a faithful **family** and church man being around so much darkness. Anybody that knows me, knows I have always been grounded in who I was and not influenced by anybody. Being in church and around my **family** has given me a solid foundation in knowing who I am, as well as where and what I come from. Those things are what has kept me throughout all the craziness and made me as strong as I am. I don't drink, smoke or be with women who aren't my wife. I don't even curse; and yet I have worked with some of the vilest dudes you can come across. But it's a silent respect there. I don't try to be who I'm not and I don't take anything away from anybody who lives their life opposite of me.

A lot of those guys didn't come up the same way I did; they've got a different background, so I don't judge them or think what they're doing is bad. I do me and they do them. I feel like my presence, being the way I am, in certain places like these clubs is an example that you can choose a different path. The crazy thing is, a majority of the people on the most drugs that I'm around, brag to everybody else that I don't do any of that.

Now that I'm older, I hope to be a role model to these young guys to look at and say, 'it might be okay to be like Zaytoven and kick it like he kicks it. I want to live clean and sober.' I honestly think it's why God has me in the business that I'm in and the position I'm in; to give people something different to look at. I don't preach to anybody, I hope to inspire others or at least show that it's possible to be in this industry and not be of it.

My living is a testimony but I don't want people to get it twisted. I don't look down on anybody or treat them differently, because a lot of these guys who do the craziest things are the ones who made me popular. They played a large part in who I am today. They were the ones who shouted me out on records. I look at these guys like my extended **family**. The artists I've been around have had some of the craziest reputations; and I had them coming over to my momma's house to work, but I never worried about nothing popping off because I understand the protection I have around me.

There was a prophetess that sang a song to me while I was playing the keyboard in church one Sunday morning. She chose Aaliyah's "One in a Million" telling me that I was one in a million. I owe that favor and blessing to God and my **family**.

Family is everything. Make sure that you keep them first in your life. Doing music is cool and rewarding, but it's not worth sacrificing the relationships of the people who will be with you and give you encouragement when the world turns cold, and it will. I've been on top, winning and attending the Grammys, walking red carpets and traveling to some cool places; but I've also experienced moments, when the same people who were in my face when I was up, wouldn't return my phone calls when I didn't have a song on the radio.

It's a great feeling to be able to take comfort in your **family** and loved ones. It's priceless to be able to share your accomplishments with those people who genuinely care about you. Don't forget to create a life while in pursuit of your career.

I'm just Zaying…I always try to make deposits of quality time into the account known as my **family**. Because my job can be time consuming and my schedule can change at the last minute, I don't worry about a low or negative balance because I keep that account in excellent standing. On the occasions I need to make a withdrawal (like a last minute flight to LA), the account is so full that my wife and kids understand. When I get back in town, I make sure I make an immediate deposit. In an industry like this, having a peaceful home environment is priceless. I've found that when I take care of **family** first, everybody is joyful, they support me in all I do and my business thrives.

He sleeps at night, is up and about during the day, and all the while the seeds are sprouting and growing. Yet he does not know how it happens.
—Mark 4:27

7. Grow

Growing up, I often heard the older people say to bloom where you're planted. Now that I am older, it makes all the sense in the world to me. I know without a doubt that music is my foundation, it's a steady tree of life. As I've developed my craft over the years I also realize that this tree keeps on giving me life, like scoring movies, starting a band, opening a barber shop and helping my wife launch her beauty and fashion business. Those business ventures are the branches, but they're all rooted in the same source.

Growth in life is vital. You've got to keep moving, otherwise you're dead. Maybe not literally, but emotionally, spiritually and mentally. If you don't choose to get going, you will be forced to move and that direction may take you someplace you don't want to go. I'm not sure about you, but I'd rather decide my path. The thing about the entertainment industry, or really entrepreneurship, is that you must constantly change and reinvent yourself to stay relevant (more on that later). One of the ways I grew was by creating multiple streams of income. I have always believed in investing in myself and have been willing to put my money where my passion was. I sacrificed a lot to get to this point in my life but looking back, the returns have definitely been worth the risks.

Grow where you are. I took the things that I was passionate about and figured out various ways I could make money. I am confident that since you're reading this book that you're serious about your career and also a believer in investing in yourself. That's where it all starts. It just takes that first step to get **growing**.

There was a time when my name was cold, then super hot, then mild, then cold and back to super hot. But I've always been a level-headed guy and used my down-time wisely. Through the relationships I had made years ago and by remaining humble, I stayed relevant by working with rising talent like Future, Scooter and 2 Chainz; but my work on their projects was light. I didn't have the same radio presence I once did. Instead of remaining stagnant and beating a dead horse, I got out of my comfort zone and tried something different. But I kept my ventures close to my natural talents. I always wanted to score a movie; but since nobody was ringing my line to do it, I made a movie where I could provide the soundtrack. With the help of writer and director Al Nuke, we made it happen.

I frequently ask myself the question, 'What else can I do with the skills and connections I have right now?' It's a great way to get your mind to think of new ways to **grow** from where you currently are. I asked myself that question when I had some idle time putting together a Rocko and Gucci mixtape. I had Al shooting some behind-the-scenes footage of us working in the studio, but the mixtape project stalled.

By asking ourselves what could be done immediately with the footage we had shot, Al came up with the idea for *Birds of a Feather*. That's just how it happened. Don't wait for other people to feed you, find a way to sustain yourself. You have everything you need right now to get you everything you dream of. Keep going, keep **growing** and then **grow** some more. Plant seeds (come up with ideas and goals) and water them (work diligently daily) and repeat that process. If you do those 2 things, you will always be fed.

I'm just Zaying…One of the ways I continue to **grow** is by having mentors or what some people may refer to as 'life coaches.' But regardless of what term you use, having someone on your side who has been where you're going is essential to your development. And you don't have to have just one mentor. I have three—a spiritual, business and financial coach. They each serve a specific area in my life that allows me to **grow** in ways I wouldn't be able to without their guidance.

Let us not become weary in doing good, for at the proper time we will reap a harvest if we do not give up.

—Galatians 6:9

8. Habit

Since we are what we repeatedly do, what do your **habits** say about you? I have always been a routine type of guy. No matter what time I go to bed, I generally get up the same time every morning, which is around 6 because I like to take my kids to school. And because I have young children, it forces me to have to work around their schedule and be impeccable with my time. I also come from a military background, so I'm sure that plays a part in how I prioritize my day.

But what about you? Are you the type of person who gets distracted easily? Do you work on music only when you feel inspired? How much time do you set aside to work on or study your craft? Are you going out regularly to network or attend showcases? Do you make beats every day? Are you saving and investing in equipment? Exactly what are you doing to prepare yourself for opportunities?

Answering these and similar questions is vital to understanding what you're doing right and what you can improve upon. Let your failures be your teacher as well as your successes. Simply put, get into the **habit** of duplicating the actions that yield you the results you want and discarding those that don't.

Get into the habit of being uncomfortable. I had multiple hit singles in the streets; but I never stopped the **habit** of doing things that took me out of my comfort zone. Making *Birds of a Feather* was a great professional challenge for me because I never wanted to act. I'm a music guy (and barber), not an actor. But I found myself applying the same techniques to acting as I did to making records. I **habitually** used the same proven formula. My goal was to try something new that I was interested in and if people liked what I put out, cool; and if not, then I at least enjoyed the process.

Thankfully, the film was well received and Al and I formed a production company to create more movie projects. The key is not to overcomplicate things, but try new things. Whether that's finishing a beat, putting out a mixtape, starting a business, writing a script, whatever you find yourself wanting to do, the key is to simply do it. Keep reminding yourself that you get back what you put out and you'll never reach your destination if you don't do things that put you in the game.

A thousand dope beats on your hard drive mean nothing if you're not trying to get them heard. I wanted to buy music equipment, so I got an extra job and used layaway plans. When I wanted to learn how to produce, I practiced deliberately every single day and devoted countless hours studying producers I admired. I chose to invest my time in Gucci when everyone else was telling me he would never make it. I starred in and made the score for *Birds of a Feather* when I had zero acting skills and no scoring experience. While other people were busy talking about what they were going to do, I was doing it.

I developed the **habit** of action even though I was uncertain of how it was all going to turn out. In Mark 9:24 it reads in part, *"I believe, but help my unbelief."* It's okay to be doubtful in your head. I think that's just human nature, however deep in your heart you have to believe in yourself and talent enough to step out on faith and try. If any of you follow me on Twitter, you'll know my motto is 'all gas, no brakes.' I press 'go' when I'm not sure or ready or even prepared.

Don't let excuses and fear rob you out of your greatest opportunities. If your goals scare you, then you're on the right track; and if they don't, you might want to set some higher goals. Fear is a hater, and successful people take the energy of hate and convert it into the fuel they need to get to the next level.

When I first started working with songwriter Sean Garrett I was excited about the opportunity, yet it made me nervous at the same time. He was heavily established in R&B and Pop culture, while I had developed my sound in the Rap world. I didn't want to fail. But I felt the fear and did it anyway. The result was my first #1 record and Grammy win for Usher's "Papers" single from the Raymond v. Raymond album.

Get into the habit of doing what you don't want to do when you don't want to do it. This is a major factor for indie producers in the music industry. This is not a punch-in-punch-out-8-hour-a-day job and because of that, there are no rules. Nobody is looking over your shoulder to make sure you're doing the work. There is a stigma amongst producers and artists that we're vampires; we sleep all day and stay up all night, working. That might be true for some, but not me. I go to bed late but I'm still up early whether it's to take my kids to school, take a meeting, make beats or go to the gym.

Of course I'd rather be sleeping, but I choose not to. That's why what you're doing has to be your true calling, your passion. Otherwise it's easy to not do the hard stuff, or even the easy stuff. The crazy part is I get up early and I still turn right around and spend most of the night in the studio with artists, since they prefer to work late.

You've got to decide what you want and then put in the work without complaining. Let me tell you that the results I've gotten by disciplining myself to work, even when I didn't feel like it, is why I'm able to live a comfortable life.

Get into the habit of saying 'yes'. I know a lot of people will argue with me on this one; but again, this is my personal philosophy. It may not work in all industries; but in the music game and especially when you're your own boss, you have to plant as many seeds as possible. Say 'yes' to showcases, video shoots, music festivals, listening events, producer and artist panels, as well as open mic nights. You just never know who you'll meet.

I'm not really into going out; but the next guy I need to work with or know might be at one of these events and I need to meet him. That's how I met half the artists I've worked with, by attending a club or function, despite the fact that I'd rather be at home creating. I've also said 'yes' to events and somebody ends up buying a beat from me, or interviewing me for their website or magazine.

My publicist will tell you that I don't care to go to all the functions she invites me to; but I show up anyway, and more times than not, something productive comes from it. Now everything you find out about isn't going to be worth your presence; but understand that the more face time you have with people, the better your odds are at getting a check, or at the very least, making a new connect, which can lead to a check.

I'm just Zaying… Get into the **habit** of staying consistent about consistency. Develop a solid and consistent work ethic. Stay consistent with practicing and improving your musical skills. If you start out working four days a week, keep that pace. Don't go hard for two weeks in a row and slack for a month. And get into the **habit** of making consistently good beats. I know all my beats aren't hits, but I work hard every time I'm in the studio to stay consistent and bang out some heat.

But divide your investments among many places,
for you do not know what risks might lie ahead.
—Ecclesiastes 11:2

9. Invest

If you believe in your talent, **invest** in yourself. Buy better equipment, enroll in classes to learn a new skill, build a website, have a professional bio written, buy and read educational or inspirational books; **invest** the time and money into becoming a better you. Trust me when I say you will never go wrong by doing this. Business Philosopher Jim Rohn says, *"Formal education will make you a living but self-education will make you a fortune."*

Speaking from experience, I saved money to buy my first set of clippers and once I taught myself how to cut I did it for free until I built up a clientele. After I earned enough cash, I bought better clippers and made more money because I got more clients. I did the same thing with purchasing studio equipment. It's not enough to simply say that you want to be a producer, you have to put your money and time where your mouth is. The more you have to offer, the more valuable you will be as well.

Invest in you. I absolutely live by the bible verse *"faith without works is dead."* Nobody wants to assist or **invest** in anybody that's not working and proving why they're worthy of help. It shows lack of faith or belief in yourself. If you tell me you want to be the best in this business, but I never see you out, you never have any quality product, you have no social media presence and you're always 'working' on something but I haven't heard or seen anything; and yet you stay complaining about how nobody will help you, what can I do?

Not putting in the time and work can be your greatest downfall. That's where belief comes in. Lack of confidence can kill your career before you get one. I've seen people who aren't that talented, but believe and **invest** in themselves and become successful; while I've known some of the most gifted folks who never go anywhere because they don't want to risk anything, or believe they can do something worthwhile. And if I meet those two kinds of people, who do you think I'm going to **invest** in? If I am spending time away from family, it's got to mean something; and if you're not **investing** in yourself, why should I or anybody else?

Invest in your health. If you don't feel well, chances are you're not going to do well. Part of being the best is feeling your best. Get some affordable health insurance and dental coverage to maintain your good health, and in case something happens. It's not as expensive as you may think either. There are a variety of plans with reasonable and affordable rates to fit most budgets. There are enough stressful situations and legitimate worries to occupy your mind, but don't let the lack of having health and dental insurance be one of them. If you fall out somewhere or have a dental emergency you'll be prepared to deal with the challenge.

Having money means nothing if you don't have the good health to enjoy it. And keep your body in good shape too. Playing ball helps me stay fit and it also allows me to release tension. If a membership to a gym isn't in the budget, walking and jogging around your neighborhood is free. No excuses. Take care of your health.

Invest in others. When I met Gucci, Yung LA and OJ, I didn't have anything to gain at first, it was all about me believing in them. I **invested** the highest commodity we all have which is time. Since I knew I couldn't get that back, I made sure that every minute we were scheduled to work, we did just that. If we were out, I was networking. I made sure that I got some sort of return on my **investment** each time we linked up.

Invest in essential marketing materials. Secure your domain name for you and/or your company and build a simple website. As I mentioned before, once you've selected your producer name, secure it and on social media also. And keep the spelling consistent. Do a quick search to make sure the name you pick isn't taken or used by someone in the identical field.

Your bio. A bio is an important selling tool if done right. Many times journalists don't have time to do a proper interview so they'll lift quotes and paragraphs from your bio to write the article. It's a cool way to control your own message. Spend the money on a good bio.

Good images. Spend the money. Like the bio, your images will be seen in print and online, and possibly TV; so make sure your pictures are high-quality, hi-resolution by editorial standards, which is generally 300 dpi. To start, make sure you have a good head shot and a full body picture. Also keep the seasons in mind if you're just doing one look. If you're wearing a coat in your photo shoot, yet using the pictures for a good portion of the year, you might want to reconsider your wardrobe choices. I would suggest doing two looks, that way you have options. And another note. I know a lot of people like to be artistic in photos; but make sure you show your face, especially if you're new on the scene. The purpose is to get people familiar with you, so keep that in mind.

*I'm just Zaying...*I saw an Instagram post that said something like— you can't cheat the grind, it knows exactly how much time you've put in. Don't cheat yourself. That kind of mentality only holds you back. Whether you are self-employed or work in corporate America, you should think of yourself as the boss, because in essence you are. You are the boss of you! So when you think you're getting ahead by **investing** less time, quality and effort, but demanding the same pay, you're only fooling yourself. It will only be a matter of time before your lack of integrity will catch up with you. Don't settle. Don't accept mediocrity. Don't get comfortable with comfort. Go the extra mile. Be excellent. **Invest** in your future.

Show me someone who does a good job, and I will show you someone who is better than most and worthy of the company of kings.
—Proverbs 22:29

10. Job

If you treat your **job** like a **job** it will pay you like one but if you treat your **job** like a hobby it will pay you like one. Think about it like this: Would you support a business or businessperson that wasn't competent, didn't have a professional website, didn't improve upon the services they offered, didn't have any hours, never answered the phone or returned calls, expected you to pay without doing a good **job** or providing great customer service or showed up late to scheduled appointments? Whether you work for yourself or someone else, you're a BOSS. You don't have to have the title to be a leader. You're the boss of you and everything you do or don't do is a reflection of the company, which is you.

Don't party on the job. It doesn't matter if I'm playing for the church or have a studio session with a rapper, I try to be as professional as possible. I think it helps that I don't smoke or drink. I've seen artists who start off respecting somebody they're paying for a service only to turn around and start chumping them off. They get too comfortable and the artist doesn't see them as a professional anymore because they're doing the same things with them.

I'm not one to judge or tell somebody what to do but I will advise that if you like to partake in the same kinds of recreational activities as your clients, do it on your own time, even if everyone else is doing it. Separate yourself and stay in the clear. You're there to do a **job**, not be homeboys no matter how tempting the situation is. How can you expect clients to take you and your business serious if you're acting like them or chilling too hard or too much with them?

Now I'm not saying you can't be cool and I'm not saying you can't be friends. I hang out with my clients when we've got work to do or promote, but I never make the mistake of getting too comfortable. That's where your family and friends come in. Those are the people who know and care about you unconditionally. Those are the people you can be off the clock with.

Show up and work on your job every day. While it's almost impossible for me and most producers to keep consistent business hours, I do block out times in my day that I dedicate to just creating and making beats. When I was doing *Birds of a Feather*, I scheduled time where I did nothing but worked on score music. Definitely have a loose schedule, but set aside a chunk of time to get important work done.

If you don't, later sometimes becomes never. There is always something else to do. I know that firsthand. I do have some boundaries established. I never miss Wednesday night church rehearsal or Sunday morning church service and I always attend my kids important functions and family events. I can work around everything else. Identify the things that are important to you and adjust your work schedule accordingly.

I'm just Zaying… Being independent means that while you may have people around who help you out with certain tasks, if things don't get done that you ensured would, all eyes (and blame) will be on you. If you tell somebody you're going to do something, keep your word. Always see a promise through. Follow-through is part of the **job**.

Getting wisdom is the wisest thing you can do!
And whatever else you do, develop good judgment.
—Proverbs 4:7

11. Knowledge

To **know** is to have power. If you're equipped with the right **knowledge**, you can have, do and be anything you want. If you had access to an exclusive industry party with some of the top players that could take you to the next level would you **know** who they were? If showing up is half the battle, then **knowing** is the other 50%. It doesn't matter if you go to all the right functions, if you don't **know** who to talk to or what to say, as well as not say, you might as well stay home.

You need to **know** how your industry works, the trends, what artists are looking for beats, what the latest equipment is, who the new producers are, what your target client or audience wants to hear. They don't call it a grind for nothing. You've got to do your homework and consistently stay prepared. And for whatever you don't **know** ask, research or read a book on the subject. To not **know**, especially in this digital era and with search engines like Google at your fingertips, is inexcusable. Stay on top of what changes are being made in the industry, **know** the language of the business. Don't be lazy in learning and getting a full understanding of how things work.

Know what you want. If you were offered an opportunity that could change your life, would you **know** it? What kind of music do you want to produce? Hip-Hop? EDM? Pop? Country? Rock? Blues? R&B? Even though I knew I could and would venture out into other genres, I made my mark in Hip-Hop. I think it's important to establish yourself in one genre first, the one you're most passionate about, before you branch out.

Don't concern yourself with being pigeonholed. People will want to work with you regardless, as long as you're making quality music. Sean Garrett tapped me to work with him on Usher's album. Jagged Edge reached out to me for beats for their project, as did R. Kelly. Organized Noize, back in the day, were mostly **known** for working with rap groups like OutKast and Goodie Mob; yet they went on to produce one of the biggest singles for R&B quartet En Vogue. If you make dope beats, the right people will come looking for you; but you must identify what you want.

Know your strengths. What are you really good at? When you answer that question, do that all the time until you master your craft. You will most likely meet success in your area of strength. Now we're all multi-talented in numerous ways but we also have a special gift that if we hone in on with laser-like focus, can unlock riches beyond our imaginations.

Know what people think of you. Reputation is everything. According to Warren Buffet, *"It takes 20 years to build a reputation and five minutes to ruin it."* What are people saying about you and your business? While it's best to maintain a good name in the streets and in the corporate offices by doing excellent work and fair business, if that's not the case ask people whose opinions you trust for feedback. The answers you receive can give you invaluable insight on how you can improve and jumpstart the process of turning your brand reputation around immediately.

Know who you're dealing with. I think because I've dealt with a lot of street guys and based off my character alone, I've always done my best to do what I said I would do and when I said I'd do it. People don't like to play about their money or time, so handle both with care. **Know** who you're doing business with and always be clear about what's expected before money changes hands. All money is not worth having. I've turned down bread because I knew from other people's experiences how certain folks got down with business that I wasn't comfortable with.

Know what you're signing. Never, ever, ever, ever, ever under any circumstance should you sign any document without letting an attorney, *your attorney,* review it first. Read that again and again until you commit it to memory. I can't stress this point enough. I've seen friendships, both business and personal, ruined all because of a signature, or lack of one, on a sheet of paper. I don't care how good something sounds or what somebody promises you or hypes you up about or how many unpaid bills you've got, do not ever sign anything without consulting your lawyer.

You would think that people would **know** better than to blindly autograph a contract after countless examples of people getting influenced, tricked or sued, but apparently not. Never let your current situation, no matter how dire, rob you out of your rights to future earnings. Don't cave in to the pressure. If that person can't understand your need for legal council before signing or if they threaten to take a deal off the table unless you sign immediately, that's a red flag… something isn't right. Be hungry for opportunities, but never starving. There are a lot of wolves out here who can smell the fresh blood of desperation. Don't be a victim.

I'm just Zaying… Be a student first. I must admit that I didn't **know** how everything worked in the beginning; but I suggest that you learn from my mistake. You can never be too educated, get all the information and **knowledge** that you can.

A wise man will hear and increase learning, and a man of understanding will attain wise counsel.
—Proverbs 1:5

12. Listen

Having two ears and one mouth isn't a coincidence. Research has shown that 80% of a CEO's salary is earned by **listening**. Knowing that, **listening** is definitely a great skill to cultivate. When people first meet me they think I'm quiet or reserved, but I'm observing. You learn more when you allow others to do the talking, especially in an environment where people are giving out game. It also helps you to separate the real from the ridiculous.

I've found that the more some people talk, the less they really know and I can deal with them accordingly. **Listening** has also allowed me to gain insight on artists that I otherwise would've missed if I was just trying to join a discussion for the sake of being included. Learn to talk only when you can add something valuable to the conversation, especially in a business environment.

Listen to music; your own, other producers, various artists in all genres. Listen to the arrangement of the beats, the sounds, the instrumentation, the lyrics, the vocals and how everything is arranged. Become not only a fan but a student of music. Music is a simple, yet complex art form. By **listening** to music it can only enhance your own ear and help you advance in your career. I have made some of the most gutter records, but I love **listening** to Gospel music. Deitrick Haddon and Canton Jones are just a couple of my favorites. By **listening** to other forms of music, it allows me to clear my mind and inspires sounds that I sometimes incorporate into my beats.

Listen to your spirit and God's voice. I've gotten so good at knowing people who have ill intentions, personally and businesswise. There are artists who I know if I work with them now, just because they're hot, will cause me problems later on. I can feel what opportunities I should pass on and when to jump on others. I think my consciousness has been sharpened over time through prayer, reading the Bible, actively **listening** in church, giving my family the time and attention they deserve and playing basketball.

I **listen** to my body. It tells me when I need to rest or change my diet, all important elements when you have a rigorous work schedule. I know friends that meditate, fast for days or weeks, run triathlons and some that drink, smoke and go to strip clubs. You have to decide for yourself what brings you joy, not just happiness. I also have young kids and I try to live my life in a way that I hope they adopt. We all hear that inner voice that tells us when we need to sit down and when it's time to make a move.

Because we producers are surrounded by sounds so much, take some time out every now and then to just be still and **listen** to nothing. Learn to be contently quiet. Some things aren't worth **listening** to anyway. I heard music producer Dallas Austin used to rent a cabin in the wilderness and shut himself off from the world in order to regroup before and after big projects. Kanye West has been known to go to great lengths to recharge his battery. He soaked up the atmosphere and culture of Japan and spent nine days there shooting the video to "Stronger."

You don't have to go off in the woods or travel to another country to relax or be inspired but it's good practice to **listen** to what your spirit and body are saying so you can live a quality life and produce quality work.

I'm just Zaying… Don't forget to **listen** to what you're telling yourself. You've chosen a tough and competitive market to be in and you'll hear criticism coming from folks who have no regard for your feelings. But sometimes your own words about you can be more cruel than the ones you'd hear from a stranger. Whenever negative self-talk begins, immediately replace it with something uplifting like a Bible quote or a positive affirmation. It's not so much what you **listen** to about you, but what you believe about you that's important.

No one can serve two masters. Either he will hate the one and love the other, or he will be devoted to the one and despise the other. You cannot serve both God and Money.

—Matthew 6:24

13. Money

Let's talk about **money**. There's a French proverb that states, *"Money makes a good servant but a bad master."* How we spend **money** and save it says a lot about us. And it all begins with our mindset. There are a lot of people who think once they get a lot of **money** they'll be able to handle it. What they fail to realize is that if they can't control the little they have now, it'll only be a matter of time before whatever fortune they accumulate is reduced back down to how they think. In Luke 12:48 God cautions, *"To whom much is given, of him shall much be required."* In essence, if you're not wise with $5,000 how can you be entrusted with $50,000? If you don't take care of the one car you have, will you take care of two or three?

Spend money on a starter kit. Because you are your business and we've talked about investing in your business, dressing well especially in this industry is a good idea. You don't have to empty your pockets, but buy the best you can afford. Also, you don't have to follow these suggestions because we all have our own opinion of fly; but use this list as a guideline to get your imagination going.

Since you'll be splitting a majority of your time between the studio (if you have sessions) and going to events, I mixed it up. Buy a nice pair of jeans (dark wash), a few good pair of shoes for casual days and business meetings when you want to make an impression, a variety of t-shirts or button downs, a few good accessories like a watch, belt, shades, a nice backpack (or for the ladies, a tote bag for your laptop) and a cologne (or perfume for ladies) that makes you feel good.

Each check you get, set aside a little bit for your starter kit fund. Even corporate professionals are told to invest in a quality blue and black suit, as well as a well-made pair of brown shoes for the same reason. The music business is no different, just a little more pretentious. And in the age of IG, looking decent is essential.

Save money. A lot of this is fun for me but at the end of the day I'm a family man with a wife and kids to think about. Whenever I get **money**, I only keep what I need and put the majority into my savings. You should never overextend yourself to the point of not being able to take care of your basic needs. If you can't afford to ball, you shouldn't be balling. Proverbs 24:27 says, *"Don't build your house and establish a home until your fields are ready, and you are sure that you can earn a living."*

While this industry is all about perception and you have to play the game to a certain extent, don't ever judge your situation by looking at somebody else's lifestyle. If a person earns $100k a year but has $99k worth of debt, he's no better off than a person that earns $40k with no or very minimal debt.

Because of my parents, I learned how not to spend beyond my means and I question everything I buy. I also pay attention to every single penny and dollar that I earn and spend. I rarely, if at all, buy on impulse because that can get you into serious debt. If something is out of my budget at the moment, I don't buy it. If I really want it, I will use one of my hustles to pay for it or I'll set aside a certain percentage to use towards that purchase until I have enough to buy it. Using this method allows me to be able to enjoy what I get without going into debt over it.

Invest your money. I used **money** I'd made over the years and invested it in a barber shop chain that I co-own called First Class, located in

Stonecrest Mall in east Atlanta. I knew that opening this business was a wise use of my resources because not only was it a business I knew all about and one that I believed in, I also enjoyed doing it. Cutting hair is a form of therapy for me. Whenever I need to escape the weight of my music life, I go to the shop and work all day. It helps to keep me grounded.

I'm just Zaying… I can be a little flashy. I like to dress and live a certain way. I was named 'best dressed' in high school; so I've been into clothes, shoes and jewelry and things like that. Although I'm not a real big jewelry person, I do have a few necklaces and watches for the cameras and I keep a new car; but I also consider some of that as an investment in brand Zay. The music industry is one big reality show and I look at it like I have a role to play. People want to see the diamonds, the rides, the clothes, the Louis V, Versace and Gucci accessories, or whatever the latest designer is. When people meet me they want to see the lights, camera, action Zay. I'd own most of these things if I wasn't in this business, but I am in this industry. It is, after all, called the ENTERTAINment business.

Our people have to learn to be diligent in their work so that all necessities are met and they don't end up with nothing to show for their lives.
—Titus 3:14

14. Necessities

The definition of a **necessity** is the unavoidable need or compulsion to do something. As a producer, an independent producer, I got tested every day when I first started, and still do. Because I manage myself, collect my own money and schedule my own time, it is an absolute **necessity** that I get certain things done and not do other things.

At first, it seems like you have all the time in the world to make beats and then when you get a few placements and start working with paying clients, you have to learn to separate wants from needs. In other words, you have to sacrifice a lot of what you want and want to do now, so you can have, do and become what you want in the future. I like this quote by St. Francis of Assisi that says, *"Start by doing what's necessary; then do what's possible, and suddenly you are doing the impossible."*

You must put in the work first, pay your dues, do your time in order to live the life you dream of. I've seen so many producers that play away their studio time by participating in activities that are not yielding them any benefits in terms of their career. And again, it's different when you manage yourself because there is no one standing over your shoulder telling you what to do and when to do it by. I've seen some big name folks who take their first big check and instead of saving or handling **necessities**, they blow it on wants and aren't able to maintain them. When you take care of your needs first, you are in essence taking care of you.

The Necessity of Building Your Name

Don't worry about getting paid for everything you do. Look at this as a form of investing in your career. Your main need in the beginning stage is to work with as many people as possible and get your name circulating. You want your name to ring bells for being talented and hard working, not hard to work with. And furthermore, if you're in this business to solely make lots of money and fast, you may need to look for another hustle.

There are a lot of people out here trying to get on, so you have to be willing to do some work for free in order to cut through the noise. It may be **necessary** to work a full-time job and do music at night or on the weekends. It may be **necessary** to sell your nice car or jewelry to finance equipment. It may be **necessary** to stay up late and get up early for months or years, in order to get work done. It may be **necessary** to downsize your whole lifestyle; and you'll do it if you want it bad enough. You've got to be willing to be uncomfortable for a while, in order to get in a position of comfort.

I'm just Zaying... You may have to sacrifice and give away a lot of music at first, in order to get where you need to be later. And be patient with it. If you're trying to hit a quick lick, stop right now. Like I said before, I'd do this for free if I had to because I like doing music that much. There are no shortcuts to success and there is no substitute for hard work. When you do what's **necessary**, your wants will take care of themselves.

Be very careful, then, how you live-not as unwise but as wise, making the most of every opportunity, because the days are evil.

—Ephesians 5:15-16

15. Opportunity

I touched on this earlier under 'Creating,' but it's such an important subject I had to dedicate a chapter specifically to it. Nothing lasts forever, especially **opportunities** and even more so in the music business. And all it takes is the right one to extend your 15 minutes into a month or maybe a lifetime.

The key is to recognize them, be prepared and seize them ASAP. Working with Gucci was that crack in the window for me and I was able to keep it open by having a slew of other artists I'd been working with lined up and ready to promote. I always had beats available for anybody looking, and I always kept CDs or jump drives with me.

Seize opportunities quickly. The one thing about **opportunities** are that they have an expiration date, which is why moving quickly is important. Playwright James Lapine put it well when he said, *"Opportunity is not a lengthy visitor."* I was at an Atlanta radio station the day before a big concert and everybody in there was trying to get at this artist who was in town for the weekend. I'd been wanting to work with him for a while and apparently so did everybody else. I'd heard him tell a few people to fall through a local studio the next day but I knew what that meant; nothing would probably happen.

When I approached him I suggested he come to my house that night. Not only did I get a single on his album, but I also sold some beats. I never want to leave anything up to chance or money on the table. Roman philosopher Seneca summed it up best when he said *"Luck is what happens when preparation meets **opportunity**."* You have to stay ready in order to capitalize on success because like time, it won't wait on you either.

As a creative person, I'm constantly coming up with ways to develop my brand. I've found that the quicker I move on an idea, the better chances I have at getting other people excited about it and carrying it out to completion. By now you know *Birds of a Feather* started off as a mixtape project with Gucci and Rocko. While we were filming the mixtape recording process, the documentary grew into a movie idea. Al and I might have said on a Tuesday that we wanted to do a movie; 10 days later Al had the script and we were shooting scenes.

Don't wait to know everything about your idea or how it's all going to come together before you act. In Ecclesiastes 11:4, it says, *"If you wait for perfect conditions, you will never get anything done."* You've got to be willing to put yourself out there and take risks. If you play it safe, chances are you're not doing anything that's going to be memorable. Remember that you get back what you put out. The bigger the risk, the bigger the reward. And just a side note, make sure you surround yourself with people who are risk takers and dreamers as well. In this business you need all the encouragement and support you can get.

Opportunities seem to favor those who are focused, excited and persistent. When you're clear about what you want and you are faithfully working on your goals every day, **opportunities** seem to show up out of nowhere. Assuming that producing is what you want to do, apply your efforts to producing, and nothing else. Don't be what the old folks say, *"a jack of all trades, but a master of none."* Your focus will determine the direction of your life. You will get what you focus on. Don't waste time, money and energy doing things that aren't moving you closer to your dreams.

I'm just Zaying... I must warn you that there will be times you seize an **opportunity** only to learn that you didn't make the right decision. But look for a way to make it work for you. There have been deals I've gotten into that ended up costing me money and I was obligated to fulfill a contract. But instead of focusing on the problem, I chose to search for ways to benefit from it, even if it was just a lesson learned to share with someone else. That one lesson is worth it, if you don't repeat it. And last but not least, stay organized. I can't tell you how many times, just having everything in order has allowed me to seize an **opportunity**.

Don't worry about anything, but in all your prayers ask God what you need, always asking him with a thankful heart.

—Philippians 4:6

16. Prayer

Prayer has been and still is the cornerstone on which I've built my career. All that I've accumulated of any real value has come to me by remaining consistently **prayerful**. And I'm not talking about material possessions. I'm thankful for the support I have around me every day. I appreciate knowing what my purpose was early in life and being able to share my gifts with the world. I am thankful for the health to enjoy what I've been given.

Prayer provides me with clarity and gives me a calmness that brings me peace, which helps me to get into my creative zone. If I wasn't creative, I wouldn't be able to make a living doing this, and for that I'm thankful. At first, a lot of people couldn't understand how I could be this church and family man, yet work in an environment that is considered corrupt by most standards.

I'm so connected to God through **prayer** that I feel like He purposefully put me in these dark places to represent a light for other people to see. I'm in no way faultless, but I do work extremely hard to lead my life by example versus trying to tell people what I think they should be doing. Francis of Assisi said, *"Preach the Gospel at all times and when necessary use words."* That quote speaks to me because I've known plenty of people who like to point fingers and condemn folks, but are the most evil people you'd ever meet. That' not me. I don't judge. That's not my job.

My responsibility is to be the best example of His glory and be a living testimony to other young people that you can be in this industry and not fall victim to temptations. And trust me, there are a lot of them; but if you want to you can resist them too.

Prayer is a privilege. **Prayer** gives meaning to everything I do and isn't limited to just a certain moment in my life. I **pray** during times of struggle and success. **Prayer** keeps my spirits up. This business can be exhausting; but whenever I meditate on God's word, I feel renewed and get the energy to keep going.

Now the cold part of all of this is the most gangster, drugged up rappers will talk to me about God and ask me to **pray** for them because they know how I am. It's a humbling honor to be able to be used in that way. Those kind of moments keep my spirits lifted and make the ups and downs I experience in the industry worth it.

Pray, meditate, get out in nature or just sit still and breathe for a few minutes and reflect on your life. Mark 1:35 says, *"And early in the morning, while it was still dark, He arose and went out and departed to a lonely place, and was **praying** there."*

Take your concerns, confusion and questions to God in **prayer**. Be patient and listen for the calming voice within to guide you. And be sure to also **pray** for those around you who may be in need of a blessing.

A producer's daily prayer. Today Lord I awaken into Your presence. I am thankful and grateful in just loving all of Your blessings. On my daily mission, please help me to always display Your spirit of love, patience and kindness, along with the gift of music that You have placed inside of me. Lord I do thank You for all this labor of love along with all the other producers and artists alike. Please allow all that read this to be inspired to live and love the art. Lord, I do realize all things are possible with You. I treasure my relationship with You. And I will always give You the honor, praise and glory You rightfully deserve. In the name of Christ today I **pray**. Amen.

*I'm just Zaying…*Jesus was known to spend all night in **prayer**. And if He felt the need to **pray**…

Let every detail in your lives—words, actions, whatever be done in the name of the Master, Jesus, thanking God the Father every step of the way.
—Colossians 3:17

17. Quality/Questions

Aristotle said, *"**Quality** is not an act, it is a habit."* When I first started producing, I might make 10 beats in a day. When I got great at it, I made 10 beats a day. The difference was **quality** that came with daily practice and consistency. Making good music has become second nature to me. I usually dedicate the early part of my day to making beats because I don't have as many interruptions and most of the guys I do business with are still asleep. But it doesn't matter what time of day you work, when you go into the studio give it all you got. Strive to produce the best possible work you can, every single time. Compete with yourself.

Quality also affects price. Until you build a solid reputation and demand, you might find yourself negotiating your rate; but how much of a discount you give depends largely on the **quality** of your production. You don't want to be known for making cheap beats. You've got to decide what you want to be known for and what kind of artists you want to work with.

I've found that people don't mind paying for **quality**. When I first started, I charged $50 for beats. I moved up to $500. My $50 beats were cool, but my $500 beats were better. Concentrate on **quality**, not quantity.

You'll make more money and reduce your workload if you sell three outstanding beats for $5k/each versus 10 mediocre beats for $1k/each. Work hard, yes, but work even smarter.

Fools are headstrong and do what they like; wise people take advice. Proverbs 12:15

Questions. Whenever I get stuck, I start asking myself and others questions. I couldn't skip this alphabet without mentioning this. Asking the right **questions** at the right time can take you where you want to go. Jim Rohn said the key to solving any problem could be found by asking yourself three **questions,** *"First, what could I do? Second, what could I read? And third, who could I ask?"*

I learned early to never assume anything. It helps you to avoid drama and misunderstanding, which can cause a lot of problems in this industry, especially as an indie. If you don't understand something or need clarification, ask **questions**.

Before you settle on being a producer or anything in the entertainment industry, ask yourself what you're doing, why you are doing it, what you want to accomplish, and how you will go about achieving success. Ask yourself what you want your life to look like. Ask these **questions** prayerfully, think deeply and don't move forward until you are satisfied with your answers. Contrary to popular belief, the only dumb **question** is the one you never ask.

*I'm just Zaying…*Always go the extra mile and treat every project you work on with the same standard of high-**quality**, whether it's for an indie or a major label artist. Why? You are the boss, so whatever work goes out is a direct reflection on you; and also because integrity should be part of your producer character. You never know who will hear that mixtape beat. That could be the record that leads you to your dream client. Everything you do affects everything else you do. Also, what you don't know can hurt you. Ask **questions**.

Because wealth is not permanent. Not even nations last forever. You cut the hay and then cut the grass on the hillsides while the next crop of hay is growing.

—Proverbs 27:24-25

18. Reinvent

I'm constantly looking for ways to take what I've already done and create something new or combining my past experiences with a fresh idea to bring about a new energy in my career. I call it the art of **reinvention**. I experienced a drought season in 2011 although I stayed selling beats; but it was during this time that I figured I needed to regroup. I learned to adapt quickly and saw it as an opportunity to learn, grow and change. You have to expect and prepare for those down times because it's not a matter of if they're coming, but when.

You have to position yourself in a way that it doesn't matter what's going on in the industry because you're prepared for anything. You don't have to accept just any job to stay afloat. For me, this book has been a long time coming and a labor of love, so I worked on it while simultaneously filming the movie. Both the film and book were projects in alignment with my God-given talent and passion, so I suggest that when you are **reinventing** yourself, be authentic and honest about your capabilities.

Reinvent, but you don't have to reinvent the wheel. One of the best things about being an entrepreneur is that you're already used to the art of self-marketing and promotion. When making *Birds of a Feather*, I'd never acted a day in my life. I had been in videos before, but that's not the same as starring in a lead role on the big screen. I went from scoring the film to being in it and I accepted the challenge. I loved the idea of trying something new and I equally liked knowing that I was **reinventing** the Zaytoven brand, yet remaining authentic.

A whole new generation has grown up since I made my name producing Gucci's hits; so this new exposure opened up a whole new fan base for me. I've gotten more people who come up to me about the movie than I ever did at the height of my production career. Now, people find out about my music after researching me from *Birds of a Feather*; it's truly amazing. And a blessing.

I've just completed my next movie project called *Finesse* under my film company with Al Nuke and I'm starring in and scoring that movie too. And this all came about because of **reinventing** the talents I already had, as well as discovering a few new ones. When you're in the **reinvention** process, don't let the unknown stop you from pushing forward. You will figure it out as you go along. Switch up how you do things and explore new approaches, but build on the foundation you've already established.

Reinvention can and should come in the form of your production style. I definitely think it's imperative to establish a signature sound; but once you've solidified yourself branch out into another genre that moves you. Usher's "Papers" was that record that **reinvented** my sound and got my name buzzing in the R&B market. Not only did I earn my first Grammy, but also my first #1 record. I also started getting label calls for more R&B beat submissions.

*I'm just Zaying...*Embrace the term **reinvent**; it's your friend. It's not that you are looking to be someone else. Think about it from the perspective that you're trying to bring about the life you're imagining for yourself into a tangible reality by acting like the person you want to become. When you start to carry yourself that way, adopting the mindset and emulating the behavior of your improved self, watch doors of opportunity open up.

The wise have wealth and luxury, but fools spend whatever they get.

—Proverbs 21:20

19. Save

Save money. It's really as simple as your grandmother taught you; basic common sense principles. Spend less than you earn. Pay down debt or off, if possible, and don't create any new bills. Not having a staff of people to pay is one of the ways I have **saved** money. You have to look at everything as a check and determine if it's worth it. I'll discuss the people I felt necessary to put on my team in the next chapter.

Like any entrepreneurial endeavor, you have to be mindful that every month is not going to be created equal. It's a gift and a curse. When times are good, work hard and know that it's not going to last. When times are bad, work hard and know things will turn in your favor if you stay the course.

I've had consistent months, even years, where money flowed in faster than I could count, followed by a slow cycle. Knowing the seasons of life has helped me to prioritize and take care of my needs before my wants. Even then, I have a financial plan I stick to; so I know that the basics are covered, including **savings**.

Save money by bartering. Whether you're just starting out or already in the game, swapping services can be a cost-efficient way to go, if it makes sense. I've known guys with studios who let upcoming producers work there in exchange for beats for their upcoming artists. I've heard of dudes trading anything from website and video services, to jewelry and cars for beats. Just be careful about who you barter with and get the agreement in writing.

Save time. I can't stand to waste money, but even more than that I hate wasting time. I've found that I get more done if I check off the biggest tasks on my to-do list first. I like to free my mind up so I can keep my attention on work or family. I also deal with problems as soon as they come up. It's a big time **saver.**

A few years ago I had a tooth that was bothering me to the point that I couldn't concentrate on anything but the pain. I went to the dentist and was told that not only did I have a cavity, but my wisdom teeth needed to be pulled. I took care of it immediately. Not only did I **save** time but money. That cavity could've turned into further decay forcing me to have to get a root canal and more costly procedures.

Pay now or pay more later. Don't miss the big picture chasing after or worrying about petty things that take you off your focus. I'll admit that you have to be flexible in this business, especially dealing with the nature of artists who live a non-stop lifestyle. One of the things I found helpful was to bundle several tasks into one. That way if they're running behind, I'm still being productive.

For example, if I'm scheduled to do a session downtown, I might have my publicist set up whatever video interviews that need to be done or call some people that have been wanting to meet and conduct everything from that one spot. It gets hectic but you get used to juggling everything. That's called survival. My publicist keeps a book or magazine with her and Al brings his laptop to work on scripts. We've even shot viral videos in the time we've had while waiting. We try to maximize our down moments so the hustle continues.

I'm just Zaying... I've been asked by some clients to hold beats for weeks that turned into months, all on the *promise* of getting paid. This goes back to treating your business like a business. There will be some people you have relationships with where this may work; but don't start what you aren't willing to finish. Don't get into the habit of making compromises with people unless you want to establish those types of relationships and reputation.

Two are better than one, because they have a good return for their labor: If either of them falls down, one can help the other up. But pity anyone who falls and has no one to help them up.

—Ecclesiastes 4:9-10

20. Team

My **team** is small but purposeful. I am not a fan of paying money for things or services that bring no value or serve a purpose. It's been in that vein that I have worked independently but in conjunction with an attorney (Karl Washington), a publicist (Tamiko Hope) and an accountant (XXX). Of course my family is part of my **team** but they are on different kind of payroll.

Being a hands-on person, I've never had a problem doing something outside of my skill set in order to get something done. But I realize that I can't do everything and have put people on my **team** that can help build, as well as maintain what I've already started.

One of the first things I base my decision off of, when bringing someone on board after I review their qualifications, is chemistry. I have to be comfortable with you and have positive energy. That's a must. I've always trusted my gut instincts and have never been steered wrong.

Put a savvy entertainment attorney on your team first. We've been over this already, but it's worth mentioning again. This should be one of the first people you employ, and again, get a reputable *entertainment* attorney. You wouldn't go to a podiatrist for a sore throat or take a Mercedes to a Ford dealership for service.

Hire someone that specializes in your field. This too can save you time and money in the long run. Also, don't wait until you are presented with a contract to look for someone. In the midst of excitement and a bit of anxiety, you may make a hasty decision based off of emotion rather than facts. Because my attorney is well-connected, he has helped me to get record placements and bring me business. Whenever that happens, we have a pre-negotiated agreement that we adhere to regarding fees.

When the time is right, add a publicist to your team. I met Tamiko Hope at a Gorilla Zoe listening party at the Atlanta Zoo. I remember it well because my wife had just given birth to our daughter Olivia and I was checking in with them when she approached me. There was a lot going on, so we didn't talk much; but she arranged a few photo ops and interviews for me since I had produced on the album.

I liked how she jumped right in to show me how a publicist works because, up until then, I didn't know exactly what role they played. If somebody wanted an interview with me, I'd schedule it myself. She called me a day or so later and we met up, but I was hesitant mostly because I didn't want to lock into a commitment. I also wasn't sure if I really needed her services. I decided to hire her to write my bio. She turned it around in a day and it was really good. She charged me a grip for it, but I liked how she understood my story and had me sounding bigger than life.

I still didn't hire her to do PR but we kept in touch. She'd hit me up to tell about events going on in the city and would invite me to come out and walk the red carpets. I liked her energy and her actions showed that she was willing to invest in me and be down for the **team** with no promises from me. What she didn't realize then but I wanted to be strategic about bringing her in, which I did after about 6 or 7 months when I had new music coming out and I didn't want to deal with folks calling me. Tamiko and I have been working together ever since.

A publicist is a great addition to your **team**, once you have created a buzz on your own and have something worth sharing; and when I say 'worth' I mean that the general public will be interested in knowing about. A publicist will help you develop your story and tell it. I had a few relationships with media people; but my publicist generated more interest in my projects and me.

I particularly liked how Tamiko would skillfully guide my interviews. Even though she would prep me beforehand, I would forget to make important points about who I was working with and what projects I had coming up. Many times when she did this, it prompted the writer to ask a question that lead to expanded coverage from a completely different angle. One particular time as I was finishing a phone interview with XXL, Tamiko informed the writer that I was the weekly judge of a local talent showcase. I ended up rating up-and-coming talent for XXL's "The Break" section.

A reputable publicist is going to cost you too. Prices vary, as do expectations; but a general rule to live by is *"you get what you pay for"*. If a publicist's rates are low, it may signal that their contact list is minimal, too. That's not a bad thing, perhaps you can grow together, but know what you're getting. Ask for a client list (both past and current), check out their website and know what they are expecting from you besides a monthly retainer. Communication here is key.

Have an accountant on your team. I'm fortunate to have a family member that is a certified accountant; but even if that wasn't the case, I'd still have someone on my **team**. And assuming you're making money or spending money on building your business, it is vital to be properly set up, ideally before any transactions are being done.

Get a business license and set up a business bank account, but consult with your accountant about what your first steps should be. Like my tooth incident, if you don't tackle this now you're going to have to do it later, but it's going to cost more money and time. Making sure you keep receipts and records of your financial statements and keeping them organized is part of you being a savvy businessman or woman. Don't be lazy in this area.

I'm just Zaying… Know who's on your **team** and who's just riding the bench. Everybody in your crew should be adding to you and not taking away. The smaller the circle, the easier it is to move. I've seen an artist lose out on major bread and mess up a business relationship all because he wanted to travel with a huge entourage. Now when I see dude, he's only with five or six people. Learn from other people's failures.

Behold, how good and how pleasant (it is) for brethren to dwell together in unity!

—Psalm 133:1

21. Unity

One of the things I love about living and working in Atlanta is the **unity** amongst the producers. I've seen the music community explode over the past decade and it's been a nice change of pace. Many of the new guys coming up have acknowledged my contribution to the industry and I equally admire the fresh sound they're flooding the Internet and airwaves with. I almost feel like a proud big brother because I've seen a lot of them grind their way to the top.

Unite with other producers coming up. As I mentioned earlier on, back in the day when an artist locked in with a producer they usually provided the beats for the entire project; but now you might have as many producers as you do songs. So it brings all these guys together in a way that creates a 'we're in this together' **unity**.

I've worked with Sonny Digital and had DJ Spinz host the *Birds of a Feather* mixtape. I think with me and all the producers here, it's all about respect. We know that it's enough work out here for everybody and you can accomplish more when you keep good relationships and stay open for collaborative opportunities. For me to connect with the younger guys, it helps keep my name in the mix amongst a whole new generation and I have the chance to learn new things. And a lot of them have been a fan of my work and they learn from me as well.

It's all about mutual respect and love for the artistic hustle. When those two elements are there, amazing success can be accomplished. I got to meet DJ Quick when I was in LA in 2013 and it was a blessing being that I have admired this guy's talent since I've been in music. He's the reason I wanted to produce and I got to bond with an old g in the industry. Just like he worked with guys from his hood, I did the same thing with guys like Gucci, OJ, Gorilla Zoe and Big Bank Black. They were all from the eastside, the same side of town I was on and it helped to develop the sound I have. **Unity** created that.

Embrace brand unity. If you take one finger and attempt to hit someone, not much happens because there's no force behind it. But if you take all five fingers and make a fist, you can knock somebody out. In essence, a united and talented team is more powerful than one person. That thought process was exemplified when making *Birds of a Feather*. We all were working together to accomplish a single goal and I couldn't have done that alone.

What I like to do is maintain my independence but recruit other talented people and bring them in and create a new partnership, whether that's doing a mixtape project or a film company.

I don't know his whole story, but I admire how Jay Z has applied this principle to his career. He seems to align himself with unique opportunities that interest him and that are also closely associated to his brand history. From the Life + Times website (lifestyle) and the 40/40 Club (nightlife) to Roc Nation (entertainment company) D'USSE' VSOP (liquor & lifestyle) and Rocawear (apparel), Jay has an empire state of mind. It seems that everything that he's associated with is united in his public persona.

His is a great example of businessmen working together to become powerful moguls as a unit and individually. I also admire how these young Atlanta producers have united and created a cool movement. Sonny Digital, Metro Boomin, Dun Deal, 808 Mafia and DJ Spinz, to name a few, have all collaborated with one another in a way that has brought them even more success as individuals.

I'm just Zaying...I think one of the reasons I enjoy working independently is that I don't really have to depend on anybody to do certain aspects of my job. I've always been the type that whatever I didn't know, I learned. But I can't deny how fulfilling collaborating with the right people can be.

Where there is no vision, the people will perish.
—Proverbs 29:18

22. Vision

You need a clear **vision**. If you don't know what you're aiming for or what direction you're going in, how will you know when you get there? It's almost like a GPS system. You have to know where you're going, in order to be guided there. Without inputting an address or a destination, the GPS is of no use. And the same can be said about your lack of **vision**. If you don't know where you're headed, you'll drift aimlessly through life and will be at the mercy of others to lead you. And you don't want to leave your life up to chance. Open your eyes and your imagination.

Our vision is like a magnetic force that draws things to us. This is why it's imperative that you are holding the right **vision** in your mind of what you want to bring to pass. Having a **vision** allows you to overcome obstacles when things get rough. When you know the plans you have for yourself it provides you with a sense of purpose that keeps you focused, no matter what gets thrown at you. Like the GPS example, if you miss a turn you will be rerouted, but the destination is still the same. The end result gets you where you set out to go.

I've used this technique in both my professional and personal life. I envisioned being successful in the music industry when I was in high school, but I didn't know it would be through playing in church and with rappers. I always saw my name on the Billboard charts and I also saw myself with gold and platinum plaques, as well as at the Grammys... and winning one.

It also worked in my personal life too. I have a loving and beautiful wife and two healthy and beautiful kids. Be intentional about what you want and make sure you focus only on what you want because this spiritual law works in the reverse as well. You get what you give your attention to. Because we are indie producers it is even more imperative that we have a **vision**. Since we are our own boss, as leaders we need **vision** in order to lead the company, which is us. Reread the scripture under **vision** again to understand how important having a **vision** really is.

Create a vision board. My family and I gather around the kitchen table at the beginning of every new year and create **vision** boards. We take images we've clipped from magazines and quotes we've printed off of the computer of how we want our year to look and paste them onto our cardboard posters. It's a great way to bond as a family, while also setting the tone of how we want our lives to look and feel. You don't have to wait for any particular time to do one, just do it. Look at it every day or as often as you can. My wife and I keep ours in a prominent place in our closets since we go in there daily and usually in the morning, so it helps us to set the tone for the day. My kids keep theirs on a wall next to their beds so it's the first thing they see in the morning and one of the last things they see when they go to bed.

While creating a **vision** board is a helpful tool, it's not the only tool you need. You have to throw in that 'A' word to make it all work together. Joel Barker stated, *"Vision without action is a dream. Action without vision is simply passing the time. Action with vision is making a positive difference."* Having a **vision** is essential. Action is also critical. Together they are powerful.

It reminds me of the classic cars I work on. I can have a beautiful 65 Impala frame with no engine and I can have a perfectly working engine with no car to put it in. When I combine the two, the result is a great running automobile. To get the end result you want, **vision** and action work best when they work together. A **vision** board isn't a genie. You can't just look at it and expect what you've pasted on it to materialize, you still have to put in the work. Remember that faith without work is dead.

I'm just Zaying… Even though I played a loose version of myself in *Birds of a Feather*, I still had to get into character. I had to **vision** myself back in the Bay and my early days in ATL. I had to recall going through things that happened to me over ten years ago and then act it out on camera. It felt real to me when I had the **vision** in my mind. It taught me that if I could take myself back in my mind to where I once was, I can do the same for my future. You can do it too. Use this technique to act like the producer you want to be five years from now. How are you walking, listening, talking, dressing, working, eating and acting? Really get into it and be consistent about making this practice a habit. Start acting like the person you want to be and you will become that person.

Write the vision and make it plain.
                                        —Habakkuk 2:2

23. Write

Now that you have your vision and vision board, you also need to **write** down the things you want to see happen in your life. It keeps you focused on what you really want to have, do and be. When I **write** down my goals or anything I want to accomplish, it gives me a sense of direction. It also helps me to prioritize my time and it moves me to act. If I say I'm going to complete something, I work hard to finish the job so I can move on to the next thing. I'm one of those guys that likes to have a clean plate. **Writing** things down frees up mental space that I can apply elsewhere.

Write out a producer wish list. About every year or so I compile a list of names of artists that I want to work with. I don't get extreme with it, but I do **write** down some A-1 names to stay motivated to continuously develop my sound and networking skills. Part of the fun is checking off the names. I enjoyed crossing off Usher and Drake, in addition to DJ Quick. Even though I didn't work with Quick (not yet), when I met him he told me he was a fan of my music so that meant more than anything else.

When I was building my studio, I made a list of all the equipment I needed and I kept that list even after I bought everything I had **written** down. I enjoyed seeing how far I'd come. I encourage you to do the same. Get a big vision for yourself and **write** it down. Then get out there and work at it until you check everything off the list. And keep repeating the process.

I'm just Zaying… Studies have shown that people who regularly **write** down their goals earn nine times as much over their lifetimes as people who don't. It pays to write.

24. Xavier

Life for me has always been about God and family; not money, fame or success. It's about learning, growing, evolving, improving and inspiring. I decided at a young age how I was going to live my life and I committed my plans to God and He has guided my steps. To Him be the glory. I never had to turn my back on **Xavier** to be Zaytoven. And I want other people to know that it's possible to make it as a child of God in this industry and be confident in what you do.

My story is about having a vision, writing it down and working hard and letting God do the rest. That's really my story. It's not so much about how great my gift is or how good I am, I just applied these principles I'm telling you about. For most of my life, I have had tunnel vision in what I was doing. I cut hair and I played music. That's what I've done my whole life until this day. The first money I ever made was playing music in the church in Jr. high school and I sold $50 beats here and there, as well as cut hair. Doing just those two things got me to where I'm at today.

The reason I think I'm here is a God intervention. The God factor. I just stuck to the script and stuck to the plan of doing what He blessed me to do. My hope is for you to discover your gifts, focus on them and work until something magical happens.

It is better to win control over yourself than over whole cities.

—Proverbs 16:32

25. You

What message are **you** sending out by the way **you** work, speak and interact with people? How do **you** dress? What message are **you** conveying to the industry? I ask these questions not to be judgmental, but to help **you** put some thought into **your** brand—**you**.

Before you try to get other people to cosign brand you, make sure you believe in you first. That's a lot of '**you**' but it's a necessary part of the foundation that **you** build yourself on because in this business as in life, it can be rough. And if **you** can't sell your own self on **you**, how do **you** expect other people to buy into it?

What do you call yourself? What's your brand name, your logo? When deciding, think about whether or not you'll want to be called that a decade or two from now. Will corporate sponsors shy away from your name? Is the name authentic, does it tell a story about **you** or your music? I believe a good name should be simple, but also reveal something about **you**.

Are you being seen and heard? Making videos wasn't as simple as it is now, but I made tons of YouTube and major videos with Gucci and a lot of the artists I was working with to market myself. Whenever and wherever **you** saw them, **you** saw Zay. I knew that if I didn't promote myself like an artist, I would get lost as being 'just the guy that made that beat.'

I came up during a time when producers were just starting to be the new stars. In some cases producers of hit records had a bigger name than the artist. I also branded myself by having a signature piano riff tag on my beats, so listeners were forced to know who I was when they heard a Zaytoven production. And the artists, especially Gucci, would shout me out on the songs so people started knowing who I was from that as well.

What are people saying about you? The world may be huge, but the entertainment industry is a small dot. Everybody pretty much knows everybody and people talk about **you**. While **you** can't control what people say and **you** certainly can't stress over it, it helps to always present the best version of yourself. I've heard that it takes three seconds to make a first impression. Every time **you** have an encounter with someone **you** have the opportunity to leave an impression. Make sure it's a good one. **You** never know who's watching and who's talking or in today's digital age, who's texting, taking pictures or recording.

Whether you've made no records, 1 record or 1,000, always keep in mind that you are a brand. I know it's cliché these days, but it's a fact. Keep all your branding efforts consistent, especially in the digital world. While I use different names on Twitter and Instagram (only because someone else had one of them before I did), it makes it easier for people to find **you** and stay informed on brand **you**. And be mindful of what **you** post on these social networking sights. If **you** lead a different life outside of work, by all means create a new page for your personal persona; but even then it's still a fine line in what **you** should Tweet and post. People often think with their eyes and hear by what they see, so be aware of what you're projecting.

I'm just Zaying...In Samuel 16:7 it states in part that, *"Man looketh on outward appearance, but the Lord looketh on the heart."* So we need to take care of ourselves for our work on earth and our spirit for God in heaven. Image is crucial.

26. Zaytoven

Z is for Zaytoven who is all about the lights, camera and action. Xavier Dotson is the guy that wants to go to the movies with his family and take his son to football practice. Deep down inside he's just an ordinary, simple person who takes pleasure in the simple things. He's actually boring and doesn't like to do a lot. Xavier is not exciting.

However when it comes to **Zaytoven**, there are so many people that know the name and want to put cameras in his face or want to talk to him or are inspired by him because he's their favorite producer. It's a different story.

Zaytoven is cool with that. He's flossy and flexes. **Zaytoven** gives the people what they want to see so he puts the glasses on and the jewelry and he's acting and moving around a certain way. **Zaytoven** has a different swagger. Xavier Dotson is the guy you walk right past and won't notice him because you're trying to get to **Zaytoven**. And while their personalities clash, they are one in the same.

Z End!

About the Author

Xavier Dotson, better known as Zaytoven is an American DJ and record producer. He was born in Germany on an Army base, was raised in San Francisco, and later moved to his current home-base Atlanta, Georgia. He has worked with Gucci Mane extensively, contributing at least one song on every one of his albums, and doing many mixtapes with him. He has also worked with other notable Atlanta artists, such as Soulja Boy Tell 'Em, Gorilla Zoe, Young Jeezy, OJ Da Juiceman, Usher (for the singer's top 40 hit "Papers") Migos (for their Hot 100 hit "Versace"), and other non-Atlanta artists such as Nicki Minaj, producing hundreds of songs in total. On June 25, 2013 he released the Independent film Birds Of A Feather with co-stars Al Nuke, Gucci Mane and Big Bank Black. In 2013 He also released the straight to DVD Movie Series *Weed Man* with co-stars Villa Mane and Str8 Dropp Tha Prophet.

Xavier resides in Atlanta, Georgia with his wife and two children.

CPSIA information can be obtained at www.ICGtesting.com
Printed in the USA
BVOW06s0456251115

428171BV00007B/156/P